on **sea**

This edition produced in 1995
© Aladdin Books Ltd 1994

Designed and produced by
Aladdin Books Ltd
28 Percy Street
London W1P 0LD

ISBN 0 7496 1701 2 (Hardback)
ISBN 0 7496 2286 5 (Paperback)

First published in
Great Britain in 1994 by
The Watts Group
96 Leonard Street
London EC2A 4RH

Design
David West
Children's Book Design
Designer
Steve Woosnam-Savage
Editor
Suzanne Melia
Picture Research
Brooks Krikler Research
Illustrators
Alex Pang
Ian Thompson

Printed in Belgium

new TECHNOLOGY

transport
on land and sea

NIGEL HAWKES

GLOUCESTER PRESS
LONDON · NEW YORK · SYDNEY

CONTENTS

NEW BICYCLES	6
MOTORCYCLES	8
SMART CARS	10
ECONOMY CARS	12
F1 ROAD CAR	14
TRUCKS AND BUSES	16
MAGLEV	18
CATAMARAN	20
YAMATO 1	22
SUBMARINES	24
AQUATAIN	26
CHRONOLOGY	28
GLOSSARY	31
INDEX	32

Photocredits
Abbreviations: t-top, m-middle, b-bottom,
l-left, r-right
Cover tl, 4b, 10t, 15b: Renault UK; cover tr,
11bl&r, 12t, 13l, 15t, 16m, 17 both: Mercedez
Benz; coverm, 4t, 5, 7b, 12m &b, 14b, 18 all, 20t,
22-23, 24-25: frank Spooner Pictures; cover b, title
p, 6-7m: Lotus Cars UK; 6b: Sinclair; 8 all: BMW;
11m, 13r: Volvo; 10b: Extension 2; 11t:
Cambrigeshire City Council; 14t: Williams Renault;
20b: Hoverspeed; 21 Three Quays; 28t: Roger Vlitos;
28m, 28-29B; Hulton Deutsch; 29t &m, 30t; The
Science Museum; 30b: US Navy.

INTRODUCTION
N E W   T E C H N O L O G Y

Travel and transport is one of the fastest growing industries in the world today. By road, rail and sea, we travel further and faster than any previous generation would have believed possible. New forms of transport are constantly being developed, to provide more convenience, comfort and speed. But if we are to meet tomorrow's transport needs without running out of fuel or polluting the Earth, plenty of new thinking will be needed. This book explains the very latest ideas in cars, buses, ships and trains: the ideas that will shape the transport networks of the future.

NEW BICYCLES
CHANGING CONCEPTS

The shape of the bicycle, unaltered for nearly a century, has been transformed in the past ten years.

New materials, new designs, and wind tunnel testing have made bikes lighter, stronger and faster. Designing bikes is rather like designing aircraft: both have to minimise wind drag, maximise efficiency, respond quickly to the controls, yet be as light as possible. The key to the bike is the frame. Nowadays, the frame of a racing-bike is made of aircraft-grade aluminium alloy, the gears of titanium, and flat discs are used instead of spoked wheels to reduce wind resistance. Brakes and gear mechanisms may be combined so less time is needed to switch from applying the brakes to changing the gears.

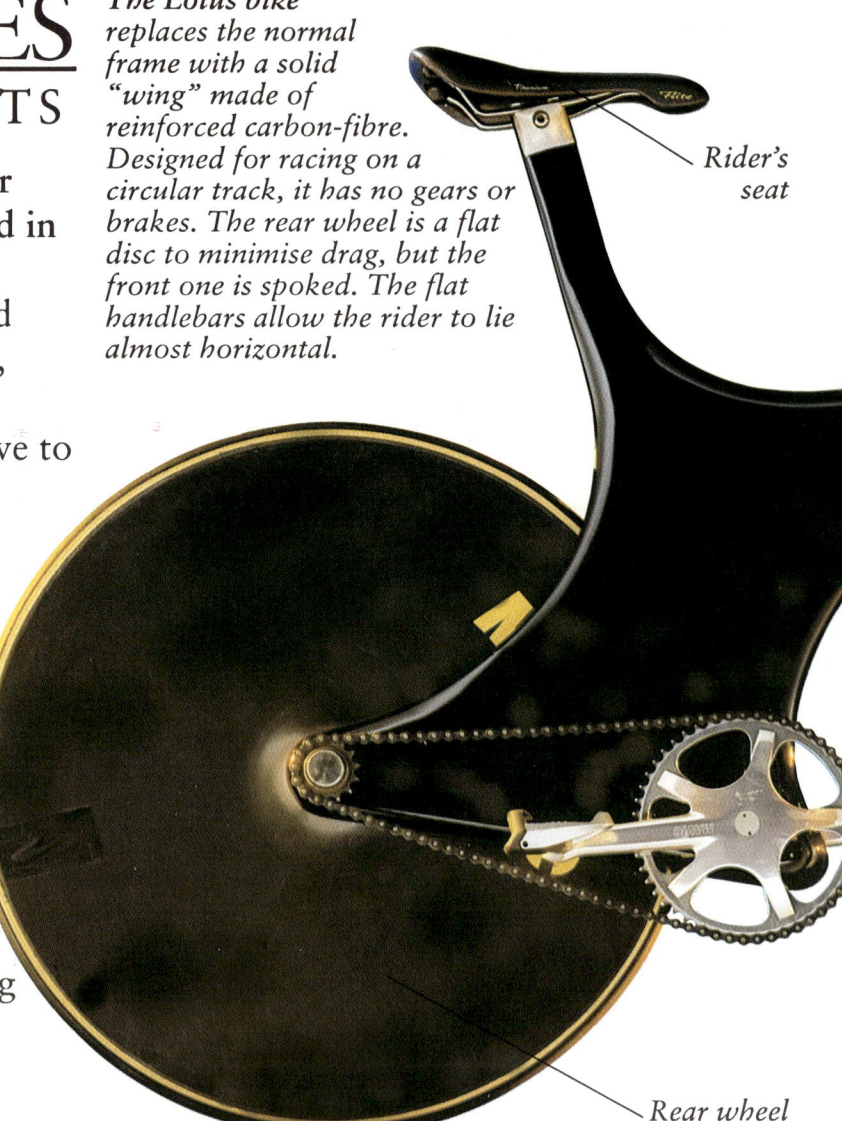

The Lotus bike replaces the normal frame with a solid "wing" made of reinforced carbon-fibre. Designed for racing on a circular track, it has no gears or brakes. The rear wheel is a flat disc to minimise drag, but the front one is spoked. The flat handlebars allow the rider to lie almost horizontal.

Rider's seat

Rear wheel

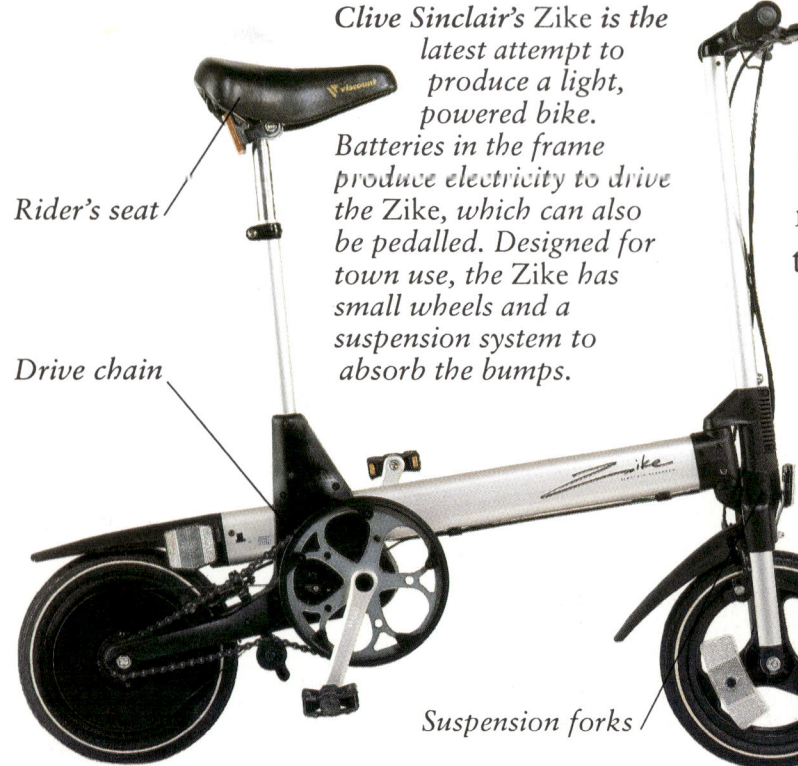

***Clive Sinclair's** Zike is the latest attempt to produce a light, powered bike. Batteries in the frame produce electricity to drive the Zike, which can also be pedalled. Designed for town use, the Zike has small wheels and a suspension system to absorb the bumps.*

Rider's seat

Drive chain

Suspension forks

Handlebars are a key factor, because they control the position of the rider. The lower the rider, the less wind resistance; but careful wind tunnel testing is needed to create optimum airflow. Riders in races like the Tour de France use drop handlebars with a curved horseshoe-shaped bar on top, which they can tuck their elbows behind for sprinting. These became popular after American cyclist, Greg Le Mond, won the 1989 tour using them. Clipless pedals, which operate like ski-bindings, are safer than the traditional toe-clip.

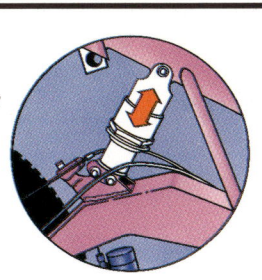

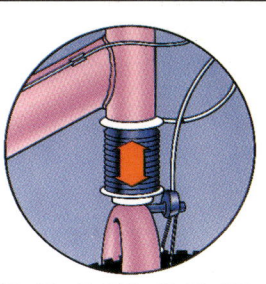

The most expensive mountain bikes, like the Cannondale Super V, *use air-sprung shock-absorbers to soak up the bumps. The movement of the front suspension can be adjusted.*

Solid "wing"

Three-pronged front wheel

SAILING ON A BICYCLE
HOW THE LOTUS BIKE WORKS

Most bikes lose speed in a cross wind. This is because drag increases sharply when the air is flowing past them at an angle. The *Lotus* bike, by contrast, is designed to go faster in those conditions by using its flat frame as a sail, taking advantage of the wind.

To achieve this, the whole bike was put into a wind tunnel with its rider, Chris Boardman, in the saddle, and wind resistance was measured at different angles. By adjusting the shape and curvature of the frame, and ensuring that it and the solid rear wheel acted as a unit, it was predicted that on a circular track, a fraction of a second would be gained every lap. Boardman went on to win an Olympic Gold at Barcelona. The precise position of the rider, allowing air to flow between him and the bike, was also perfected.

The world's oddest bike is Behemoth, *designed by American, Steve Roberts. It has 105 gears, carries four computers, a satellite navigation system, a fridge and solar cells to keep them all going. Behemoth – it stands for Big Electronic Human-Energised Machine Only Too Heavy – is a mobile office on which Roberts has pedalled 32,186 km across the United States.*

MOTORCYCLES
FASTER AND SAFER

The quickest way through the traffic is on a motorcycle. But while cars have been getting safer and more economical, motorbikes have gone the other way. Better and better performances from bigger and bigger engines may be exciting, but fuel economy has suffered. A typically modern "superbike" has an engine as powerful as most cars, and does no better than 14 km per litre. Meanwhile, little progress has been made towards creating a safer bike, or one that protects the rider from the cold and wet. "A rider simply gets colder, wetter, and uses more fuel on a bike than in a car", says British motorcycle enthusiast Royce Creasey, who designed his own improved machine, the *Voyager*.

The safety of the C1 is provided by a strong aluminium space frame, made of tubes welded together. In a crash, this would distort in a controlled fashion, providing a motorbike for the first time with "crumple zones" just like those of a modern car. Computer simulation shows that the C1, in fact, provides the same protection in a head-on collision as a small car. The frame would also protect the rider from glancing blows and prevent him being thrown over the handlebars, a major cause of serious injury.

The BMW C1, a prototype machine, protects the rider from the weather with a full roof and the option of fitting side panels for long journeys. Anti-lock brakes and an air-bag can be fitted, and there is space for 50 litres of luggage. Most car journeys are short (an average of just six and a half kms) and are made alone; perfect for a motorbike.

Rear wheel

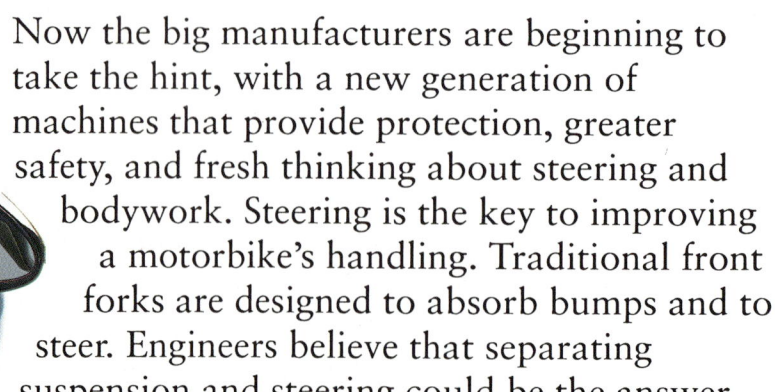

Now the big manufacturers are beginning to take the hint, with a new generation of machines that provide protection, greater safety, and fresh thinking about steering and bodywork. Steering is the key to improving a motorbike's handling. Traditional front forks are designed to absorb bumps and to steer. Engineers believe that separating suspension and steering could be the answer

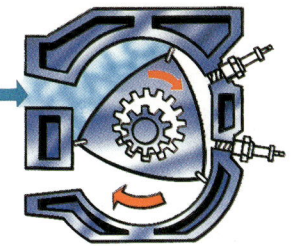

The rotor draws the fuel through the inlet port, and into the cavity.

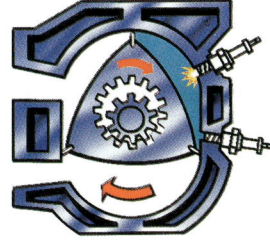

As the rotor continues to turn, the fuel is squashed into a smaller space. The spark plug fires.

The burning fuel expands into the larger space beyond the plugs, driving the rotor round. As the rotor turns, it exposes the exhaust ports, and the burned fuel escapes.

THE WANKEL ENGINE
HOW ROTARY ENGINES WORK

The ultimate engine for a motorbike is one that does not vibrate as pistons and connecting rods hurl themselves to and fro thousands of times a minute. Such an engine was designed in 1956 by German engineer Felix Wankel, and fitted in the late 1980s to the *Norton Commander*, claimed to be "the smoothest motorcycle in the world". The Wankel engine has a triangular rotor, geared to the driveshaft, and rotating in the combustion chamber. As it turns, the rotor draws in fuel, compresses it, ignites it and finally exhausts it like a normal four-stroke. It works: but wear at the rotor tips, poor fuel consumption and high emission levels count against it.

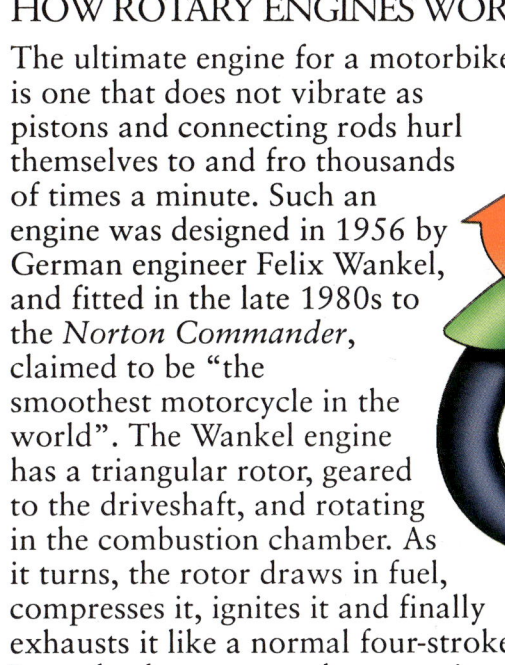

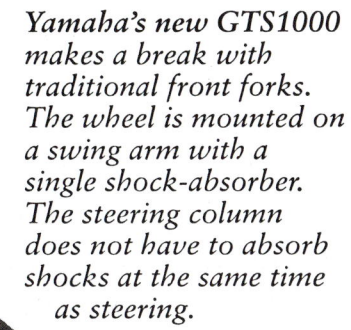

Swing arm

Yamaha's new GTS1000 makes a break with traditional front forks. The wheel is mounted on a swing arm with a single shock-absorber. The steering column does not have to absorb shocks at the same time as steering.

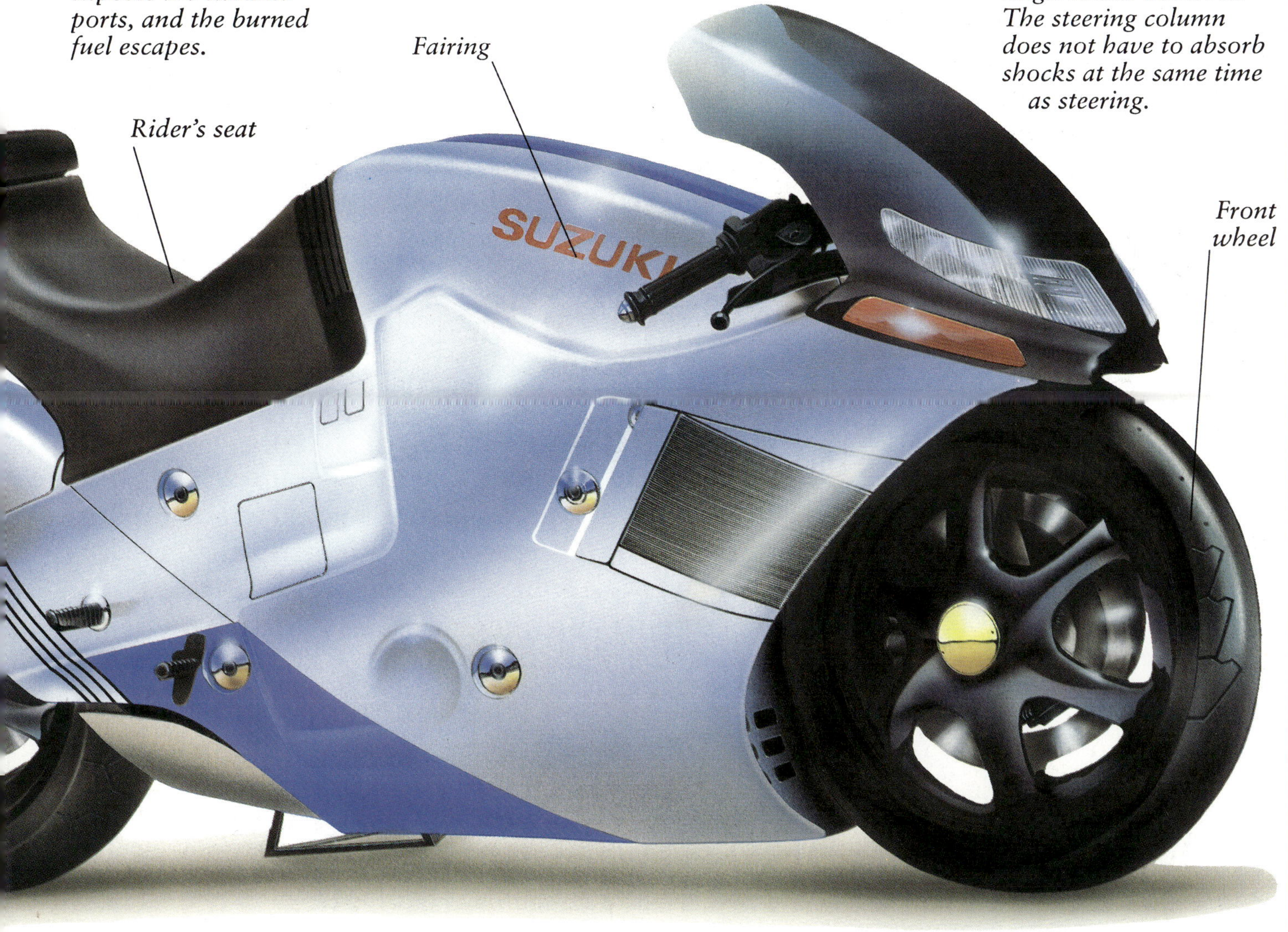

Fairing

Rider's seat

Front wheel

SUZUKI

One of the greatest problems with cars is finding somewhere to put them. Renault's concept car, the Matra Zoom, gets around this problem by making itself smaller, tucking its rear wheels under itself for parking, and stretching them out again for the open road. Other manufacturers, such as Volkswagen, have turned to electronics. Its concept car, the

Futura, is fitted with lasers and ultrasound sensors to measure the space, and to park the car.

Matra Zoom

Driving position

Parking position

Route-planners linked to a central computer will guide the driver. In a strange area, the planners will suggest the best route. At home, where routes are familiar, they will warn of road works, congestion and accidents. Systems like these are already being tested and could be common within about five years. The dashboard of the future will be designed to provide lots of clear information. Speed, fuel level, and warnings of dangers ahead may be displayed on the screen, close to the driver's line of sight.

SMART CARS
DRIVING MADE EASIER

The car of the future will make driving easier and safer.
Onboard computers will control many parts of the car, including the suspension and anti-lock brakes. Communication links will provide driver information.

Once on a motorway, cars will be driven automatically a few metres apart, using sensors to prevent crashes. This technique, called "platooning" and already tested in California, is safer and makes much better use of roads. If someone pulls out unexpectedly, all the cars will automatically slow to prevent a crash. Onboard route maps will show the way, or direct the driver by voice control. Each car will be centrally monitored, with systems that can override the driver.

Driving in the future is unlikely to be free. Some of today's road and fuel taxes will be replaced by "road pricing" systems, which will charge for the use of busy city streets or motorways. The ADEPT scheme, being developed by 16 European countries, uses beacons on the roadside and meters in the cars to deduct payments from the user's "Smart card". Charges could be based on the distance travelled, limited to a city centre, or levied only when the roads are congested. The congestion meter would be activated by microwave beacons located on the outskirts of the charging area.

THE AIR BAG
HOW LIVES ARE SAVED

Air bags are triggered by the rapid deceleration in a crash. Instantly, a small explosive charge fires, inflating the bag with gas. In a 48 km/h crash into a solid barrier, the charge fires in under ten milliseconds – blinking the eye takes fifteen times as long. By 20 milliseconds, the driver is moving forward and the bag is expanding fast. At 80 milliseconds, the car has stopped dead and the driver's head has hit the air bag, which vents gas to absorb the energy. The driver bounces back unhurt. Air bags were developed in United States where many people were (and still are) reluctant to wear seat belts. It was important to develop a restraint that was automatic and did not rely on the drivers remembering to use it. Combining the air bag and seatbelt will virtually eliminate serious head and facial injuries, even in the faster crashes.

Seat belts have cut road deaths dramatically, but not everybody wears them. Even when they do, they do not offer complete protection. In frontal crashes at 32 to 48 km/h, almost a third of drivers hit their heads on the steering wheel even if they are belted up. The air bag prevents this, inflating in a fraction of a second to provide a soft cushion, absorbing the impact of the crash. Air bags are a masterpiece of engineering, although there have been a few problems. Some materials are known to burn due to the friction caused by the inflating bag.

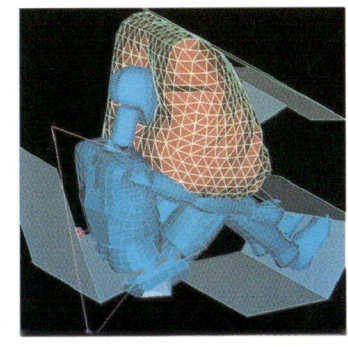

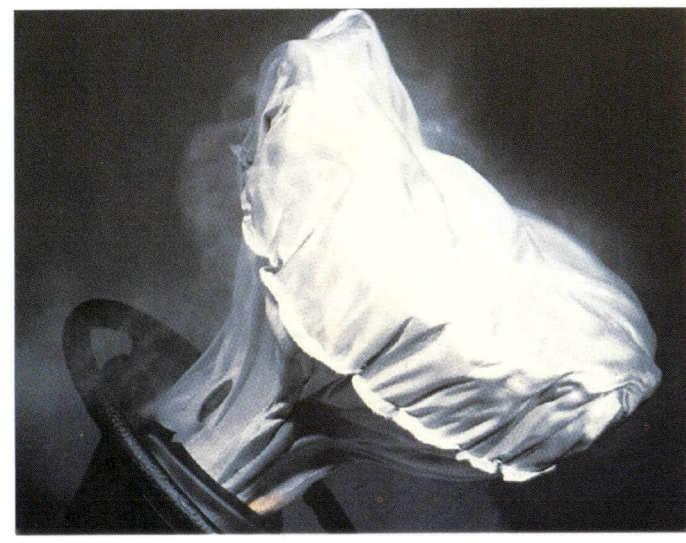

The Concept 92 car, designed by Geoff Matthews of Styling International, is supposed to be practical as well as green. The body panels would be made of plastic and attached to a frame, making it light and easily made. The weight of a car is second only to the engine in determining economy. Plastics are light, but do not degrade: an advantage to the owner, who would not have to worry about rust, but a long-term problem, as it is quite difficult to dispose of such cars at the end of their lives. The engine in Concept 92 is designed to be removed as a single unit for repair, while the owner drives away with a temporary replacement.

ECONOMY CARS
NEW TYPES OF POWER

Electric cars are waiting for one thing: a battery that can store as much energy in as small a space as a tankful of fuel. Many electric cars have been built, from Clive Sinclair's modest C5 to BMW's sophisticated E1, but all lack either speed, range, or storage space – the batteries are so large they take up most of the car. Today's best electric cars, such as the E1, are capable of 120 km/h. Now car designers are looking at hybrid cars, which combine electric motors with small engines, as the best hope of meeting the tough emission standards that are needed to clean up the world's busiest cities.

The Ultralite, a concept car, is fitted with gull-wing doors. In fact, such doors are very impractical. More sensible is the car's low weight and very small frontal area.

The Ultralite, is a streamlined car designed to use much less fuel. It is fitted with a small engine running at constant speed to generate electricity to power the car, and batteries to assist acceleration.

Traditional batteries use lead and acid to store electricity: they are heavy and expensive. Batteries weighing 100 kilograms store only as much energy as one litre of petrol or diesel. Sodium-sulphur batteries, used in the E1, perform better but are very expensive: they cost about £16,000 per car. Manufacturers are working on alternatives.

Computer-aided design is used to speed the process of creating a new car. Volvo's vehicle was turned from initial drawings into a finished prototype in less than a year. Peter Horbury, the designer, says: "This is a car that can go shopping, that is recognisable, yet is environmentally friendly, and believable."

HYBRID TECHNOLOGY
A CAR WITH ITS OWN POWER PLANT

Volvo's Environmental Concept Car uses a diesel-powered gas turbine and batteries to achieve good performance and a range of 643 km. The turbine generates electricity to power electric motors, and also to recharge batteries when the car is on the move. Acceleration is modest, but a top speed of more than 161 km/h is possible, and the car is very quiet and free of vibration. Volvo believe that such a practical vehicle could be on the roads in 10 to 15 years. The main drawback is that the nickel-cadmium batteries used would cost about £14,000. The car can either run on batteries alone, or on a combination of turbines and batteries. The turbine is a clean and efficient power source, though when operating it sounds a bit like a jet taking off!

Electric motor

Gas turbine

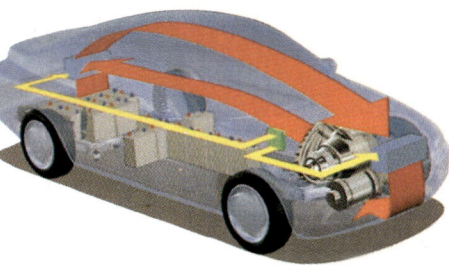

Both power sources combined

F1 ROAD CAR
USING F1 TECHNOLOGY

Formula One is the summit of the motor car, where new technologies are tested before filtering down to road cars. The modern Grand Prix car is light but immensely strong, the result of a carbon-fibre reinforced chassis that weighs only half as much as the driver who sits in it. The strength of the car comes from the curved bodywork, made from epoxy resins (a type of plastic) woven with reinforcing fibres, shaped in moulds, and then "cured" at a high temperature and pressure. Carbon-fibres are twice as stiff as metal, and don't suffer from fatigue. To keep such powerful, lightweight cars on the road, they are fitted with wings designed not to create lift, but to press the car to the road.

Williams Formula 1 racing car

After a gap of more than 30 years, Jaguar made a triumphant return to sports car racing in the late 1980s. The XJR series of cars, prepared by Tom Walkinshaw Racing, won the Le Mans 24-Hour race in 1988 and then again in 1990.

Lessons about crash-worthiness are learned the hard-way on the racing-track, but can then be applied to the road car. Two crash-absorbing beams support the front of the car. Made with several fibres, these can stretch, break or crush, absorbing the energy of the crash.

The engine forms an integral part of a Grand Prix car, bolted at the front to the chassis and at the back to the rear suspension. The Renault V10 engine, used in the Williams F1 car, produces around 700 brake horsepower (bhp), yet weighs less than 136 kg. Active suspension is designed to keep the car level at all times, reducing roll on corners, "dive" when braking and "squat" when accelerating. Each suspension unit is controlled by an onboard computer, that senses movement, and then corrects it. Semi-automatic gearboxes are controlled by switches on the steering wheel.

Ordinary wind tunnels test cars with their wheels stationary, but better results are obtained from rolling wind tunnels, where the wheels rotate. The flow of air can be assessed.

The Formula One engine is designed to run for just a single race. After that, it is taken apart down to the last nut and washer and reassembled. Renault's V10, fitted with electronic injection and ignition systems has powered the Williams team to two successive championships.

Without superchargers or exotic fuels (banned by the controlling body FISA), the output of an engine depends on how well it can breathe. Current Formula One engines have four valves per cylinder, to smooth the flow of the fuel/air mixture in, and the exhaust gases out. The engines perform best at high revolutions, which is one of the reasons why drivers spin their wheels at the start of a race.

POWERFUL ENGINES
ENGINES PUSHED TO THEIR LIMIT

The ultimate sports car is the McLaren F1, which puts Formula One technology in the hands of anybody with £700,000 to spend. Its sleek body is made of carbon-fibre, while its engine, made by BMW, is the smallest and lightest V12 ever made. The FI weighs a mere 1,018 kilograms – less than a Ford Escort – yet can reach speeds well over 321 km/h. The car's body was sculpted after extensive wind tunnel tests to ensure that its shape would stick the car firmly to the road. At the back, the F1 carries a moveable spoiler, the "brake and balance foil", which automatically rises as the driver brakes.

TRUCKS & BUSES
COMFORT AND SPEED

In the past 30 years, the truck has taken over from the train as a cargo-carrier. But truck design has moved slowly.

In Europe, the first "cabovers", in which the driver sits above or even in front of the front wheels, date from 1920. This type dominates European roads, while in the United States the driver often still sits behind the engine and front wheels. Power comes from big, turbo-charged diesel engines which provide a lot of pull at low speeds. Attempts have been made to streamline trucks. For every kilometre it travels, a big, articulated truck has to push aside 20 tonnes of air; smoothing the flow can save a lot of fuel.

SAFE BREAKING
HOW ANTI-LOCK BREAKING WORKS

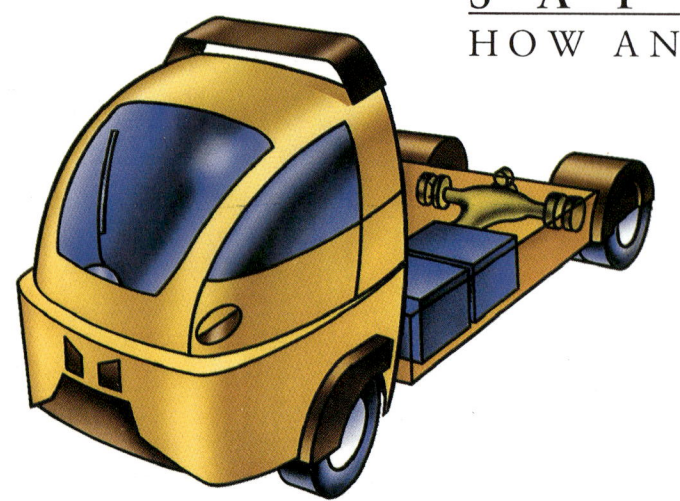

Wheels exert the greatest grip on the road just before they lock. Anti-lock braking systems work by sensing the movement of the wheels electronically, and releasing the brakes just before the wheels lock. The brakes are then reapplied and released in a very rapid cycle until the vehicle comes to a halt. Skids and jack-knifing can both be avoided. To help spread the weight they carry, most trucks have double wheels on all axles except the front.

Traditional American trucks are beginning to get a more streamlined and less aggressive appearance. The Kenworth T600B has contours designed to give better economy, including a sleeping compartment with a roof shaped as a wind baffle to help trucks carry air over the square trailer. The extra roof space makes it possible for the driver to stand up, impossible in most cabs, and air suspension for cab and sleeper increases comfort. The front wheels have been moved backwards, giving better manoeuvering ability: the turning circle is 17 metres, curb to curb. Bumper design and chassis fairings are designed to reduce turbulence.

The Mercedes-Benz super-streamlined truck is a total break with traditional concepts. The windscreen is curved, and the tractor unit integrated with the trailer to reduce drag, while the wheels are covered with panels.

First sketches for the new Mercedes 0404 coach look futuristic. The final design was less radical, but included some of these ideas.

The first buses appeared in the early 20th century, and by 1927 the coach emerged in almost its modern form – a rectangular box looking much the same from front and rear, the driver and door set ahead of the front wheels. Engines migrated from the front to beneath the floor, where they remained. The basic outline of the coach remains unchanged, though comfort, speed and safety have all increased.

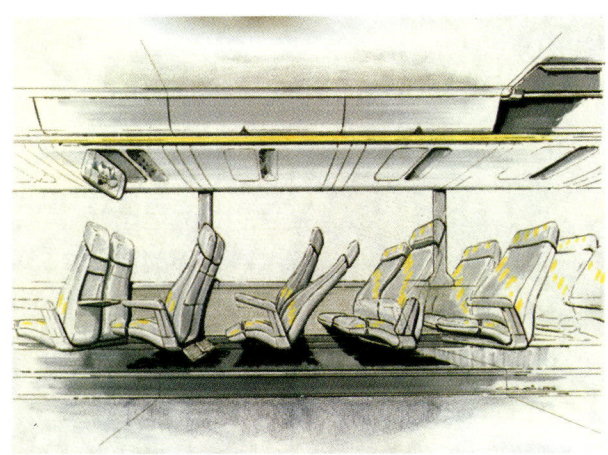

Modern coaches have reclining seats and video screens, so that passengers can be entertained in comfort. The new generation of Mercedes coaches have sophisticated suspension systems and completely redesigned seats. A scoop at the back of the roof, concealed by a spoiler, picks up fresh air for the air-conditioning system. Today's coaches have caught up with the standards of comfort of trains, and with modern roads to travel on, have become the first choice for many long journeys. There are advantages in recduced fuel consumption, but most transport companies still prefer simplicity, ruggedness and ease of servicing to saving fuel.

MAGLEV
THE NEW AGE OF TRAINS

Conventional trains, running on metal wheels on a track, can reach remarkable speeds - over 483 km/h, in the case of the French *Train á Grand Vitesse* or TGV. But even greater speeds may be possible for trains that "fly" a few centimetres above the rails, supported on a cushion of magnetism. Speeds of more than 402 km/h have been achieved by the

magnetically levitated (maglev) trains. The Japanese plan is to build a 499 km maglev track which will link Tokyo to Osaka in just one hour.

The MLU00X1 is the latest version of the maglev train designed by the Japanese company J.R.Tokai. Test vehicles run very smoothly, with only a slight whine from the electric coils, and gentle thuds caused by air pressure in the gaps between sections.

Japan has developed two distinct maglev systems. In the HSST, electromagnets in the wings of the train are wrapped around the guideway and attracted upwards towards it, supporting the train in same way. It reached a speed of 306 km/h

Sleek and aerodynamic, the MLU00X1 will also be luxurious, with a TV set for every passenger. There will also be a comfortable lounge, and a monitor room fitted with computers, telephones, and other equipment.

The French Railways, SNCF, disagree that levitation is the future of train travel. Its TGV already links the centres of Paris and Lyons, a distance of 426 km, in two hours, a time that cannot be matched by aircraft. The TGV Atlantique's record of 515 km/h is quicker than any other maglev train. When the TGV programme began in 1969, SNCF assumed that levitation would be needed to exceed 241 km/h, but its first experiments failed, and it turned back to traditional rails.

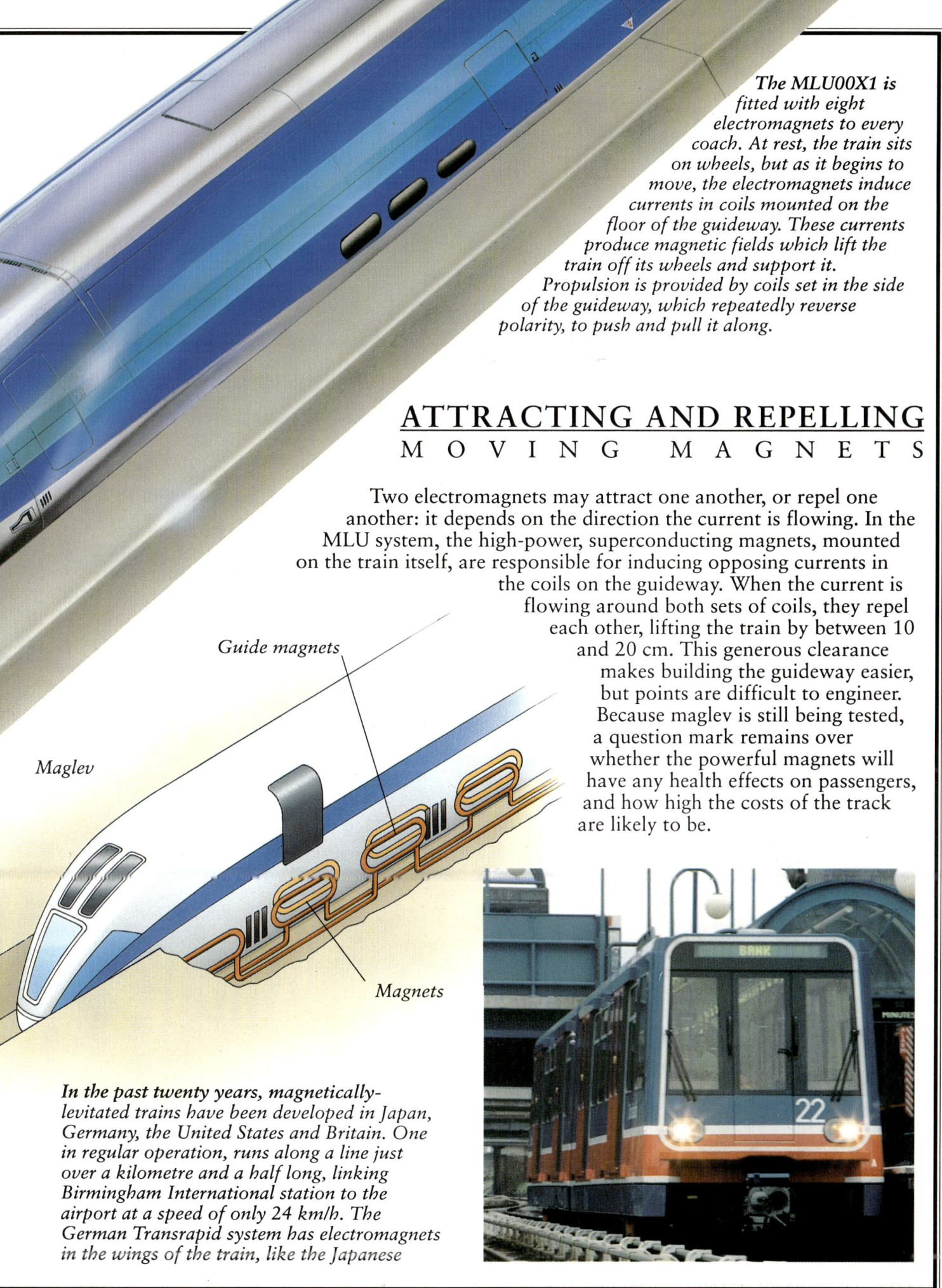

The MLU00X1 is fitted with eight electromagnets to every coach. At rest, the train sits on wheels, but as it begins to move, the electromagnets induce currents in coils mounted on the floor of the guideway. These currents produce magnetic fields which lift the train off its wheels and support it. Propulsion is provided by coils set in the side of the guideway, which repeatedly reverse polarity, to push and pull it along.

ATTRACTING AND REPELLING
MOVING MAGNETS

Two electromagnets may attract one another, or repel one another: it depends on the direction the current is flowing. In the MLU system, the high-power, superconducting magnets, mounted on the train itself, are responsible for inducing opposing currents in the coils on the guideway. When the current is flowing around both sets of coils, they repel each other, lifting the train by between 10 and 20 cm. This generous clearance makes building the guideway easier, but points are difficult to engineer. Because maglev is still being tested, a question mark remains over whether the powerful magnets will have any health effects on passengers, and how high the costs of the track are likely to be.

Guide magnets

Maglev

Magnets

In the past twenty years, magnetically-levitated trains have been developed in Japan, Germany, the United States and Britain. One in regular operation, runs along a line just over a kilometre and a half long, linking Birmingham International station to the airport at a speed of only 24 km/h. The German Transrapid system has electromagnets in the wings of the train, like the Japanese

CATAMARAN
ABOVE THE WAVES

Yachtsmen have known for years that the catamaran, two narrow hulls linked by a deck, is faster than a single-hulled boat. Now navies, ferry companies and cruise operators are discovering the same thing. The Blue Riband prize for the fastest crossing of the Atlantic by a passenger ship was won in 1990 by *Hoverspeed Great Britain*, a catamaran which covered the 4506 km from New York to Bishop's Rock off the Scilly Isles in 3 days, 7 hours, and 54 minutes. It broke *SS United States'* record set in 1952.

At least two of the world's navies have developed "stealth" ships based on the catamaran. The US Navy's Sea Shadow, a 560-tonne craft designed to carry missile launchers, has specially angled surfaces on the hull to scatter radar beams, making detection harder. The Swedish ship, Smyge, weighs 140 tonnes, has a plastic hull, and is driven by water jets rather than propellers.

The SeaCat, built in Hobart, Tasmania by International Catamarans, is designed to carry 450 passengers and 80 cars across the English Channel. Its four 16-cylinder diesel engines, coupled to water jets, give it a maximum speed of 42 knots. The twin hulls are designed to pierce the waves rather than riding over them, and to reduce the impact of the waves.

The catamaran has been used for thousands of years in the Pacific and Indian Oceans: its name comes from the Tamil word *kattumaram*, which means "trees tied together". By using two hulls instead of one, a ship can be built which is broad in the beam without being very long. The superstructure rides clear above the waves, which means that stormy seas will not sweep over the ship, though it is likely to pitch more.

This passenger catamaran, SSC Radison Diamond, is a cruise liner. It is equipped with a unique, computerised stabilisation system. Built by Brown Brothers, it controls the ship's pitching, heaving and rolling motions by the means of four fins fitted to the underwater pontoons.

R E S I S T A N C E
WHY THE CATAMARAN IS FASTER

The fastest ships are those with the longest, narrowest hulls, because that is the shape that creates the least drag. Catamarans use the same principle, except that they have two narrow hulls instead of one. A conventional liner (top) drives straight through the waves, with little buoyancy in the bows to cause pitching. This creates an easy motion, but means that waves can sweep over the ship in bad weather. The catamaran's twin hulls (bottom) hold it clear of the waves.

Ship designers use computers to perfect the shape of the catamaran. Computer-aided design is quicker, and enables ideas to be turned into prototypes much sooner. Modifications in the design can be quickly checked to see the effect.

YAMATO 1
THE MAGNETIC BOAT

For almost 150 years, the screw propeller has driven ships through the water. Now an experimental Japanese ship is challenging the supremacy of the propeller. *Yamato 1* is the first ship to be driven by electromagnetic propulsion, in which a jet of sea water is created by passing an electrical current through it inside a powerful magnetic field. The ship's construction has been financed by Japan's Ship and Ocean Foundation, which believes this form of propulsion would be ideal for military ships, fast ferries and other high-speed vessels. *Yamato 1* was built at Mitsubishi's Kobe shipyard, and has two thrusters, one designed by Mitsubishi, and the other by Toshiba. The great advantage of the system is that it has no moving parts, which means no problems of vibration, noise or wear. The layout of the ship can be more flexible, thanks to the elimination of the normal power transmission, and the reduced length of the engine-room means more space for revenue-earning cargo.

This merchant ship has been fitted with computer-controlled vertical "wings" which can be used when the wind is favourable.

In the search for other sources of power to drive ships, there has been a return to sail-power. Sail-power has been developed due to the high cost of fuel and environmental considerations. It can be combined with engine power as an energy-saving alternative.

Yamato 1 is just under 30 metres long and 9 metres wide. Its streamlined shape suggests that it is designed for high speed, but in tests conducted in 1992, it reached only a modest 6 knots when currents of 2,000 amps were passed through the sea water. Designer are trying to increase the magnet's power. Ships propelled by electromagnetism are steered by adjusting the current, and hence the thrust.

The electrical power which produces the current on *Yamato 1* is provided by two diesel generating sets, producing alternating current. This is then converted into direct current which is supplied to the electrodes. The boat's speed depends on two things: the power of the magnets and the flow of the current. To achieve six knots, 2,000 amps of electricity was needed. As the speed of the vessel increases, however, the efficiency of the propulsive system will also increase. This is why this system is considered ideal for fast vessels and for travelling long distances. It is also environmentally friendly.

MAGNETIC POWER
HOW YAMATO 1 WORKS

At the heart of *Yamato 1* is a superconducting magnet. This is made of a coil of niobium-titanium wire cooled to a temperature of -268°C in liquid helium. At this temperature, the electrical resistance of the wire falls to zero, and a current passed around the coil will continue to flow for ever, creating a powerful magnetic field. The magnets are placed around the thruster tubes which contain sea water. When a current is passed through sea water, which is a good conductor because of the salt, a force is created which drives the water out of the tubes, creating a jet to drive the ship forwards.

Suminato Heavy Industries has already made a preliminary design of a 4,000 tonne container ship propelled magnetically at speeds of up to 50 knots. The force which moves the ship forwards is just the same as that which drives an electric motor, except that in this case it is the water and not the rotor coil which feels the force and moves in response to it. The speed is controlled by regulating the current flowing through the water.

SUBMARINES
TRAVELLING UNDERWATER

The future of tourism is underwater, according to pioneers who believe that the oceans which cover three-quarters of the Earth's surface offer far greater potential than the land.

By the early 1990s, more than twenty leisure submarines were operating worldwide, with another thirteen being built. The greatest potential is in the clear water of the Caribbean, where many tourist submarines already operate around tropical islands like the Seychelles, Mauritius and Hawaii, and off the great coral reefs of Australia. One day the submarines may link up with underwater walkways, or even hotels on the bottom of the sea. Great care will be needed to protect the oceans from pollution and damage.

The tourist submarine MK 111/48 was built by the Finnish company W-Sub of Turku, and designed for use in the Egyptian part of the Red Sea, where it complements an underwater observatory. It is fitted with large windows along its entire length to give tourists the best view of life under the sea.

The sunken Titanic was found by a three-man submarine, the Alvin, which carried a 71 cm robot camera, Jason Jnr. After descending two and a half miles below the surface, Jason Jnr was freed from Alvin and took pictures while being controlled through a 61 metre cable. The robot went down through four of the liner's 13 decks, filming and recording what it saw on videotape. Delicately manoeuvering it like a helicopter with a joystick, the crew were able to discover the wreck of the Titanic.

DIVING AND RISING
HOW THE SUBMARINE WORKS

The buoyancy of the submarine is controlled by tanks which can be flooded with water to make it sink. When it is time to come to the surface again, compressed air is used to blow the water out of the tanks, lightening the submarine and making it float to the surface.

Main fin

Radio mast

Observation windows

Ballast tanks

SEABUS

Tourist submarines can carry about 50 people to a depth of 100 metres or so. Exploring much greater depths requires stronger structures, such as the bathyscaphes (observation tanks) that have penetrated the depths of the deepest oceans. But it is possible to explore by using television cameras mounted on unmanned submersibles, and controlled from the surface. In 1986, the liner *Titanic*, which sank on its maiden voyage in 1912, was rediscovered and explored. The pictures showed crystal chandeliers and brightly polished metalwork, its shine apparently undiminished by 74 years on the bed of the Atlantic.

The SPT-16, built by the Swiss engineering firm, Sulzer Brothers of Winterthur, is designed to carry 18 passengers on safaris under the waters of the Swiss lakes. Thirteen metres long and weighing 33 tonnes, the submarine is made from four welded steel sections, and has a large, acrylic viewport at the front, and four pairs of windows to ensure the maximum field of view.

AQUATAIN
THE FLYING BOAT

For years, Western intelligence officials were bewildered by a strange craft, half plane and half boat, which appeared in satellite photographs of the Soviet Union. Now the Cold War is over, its Russian developers have unveiled details of how the craft works. They call it an "ekranoplane" (from the Russian for surface, *îekranoi*) and claim that its high efficiency and low fuel costs come from exploiting something that the early flyers were familiar with – gaining extra lift by flying close to the ground or the sea. Dubbed the "Caspian Sea Monster" by American intelligence experts, the flying boat can skim the surface on an air cushion, something like a hovercraft, but can also soar thousands of metres upwards to avoid bad weather. *Jane's Defence Weekly* published the first photographs of this Wing in Ground Effect craft (WIG), and it was immediately recognised as a spectacular piece of technology. The "ekranoplane" can fly over water, land or ice.

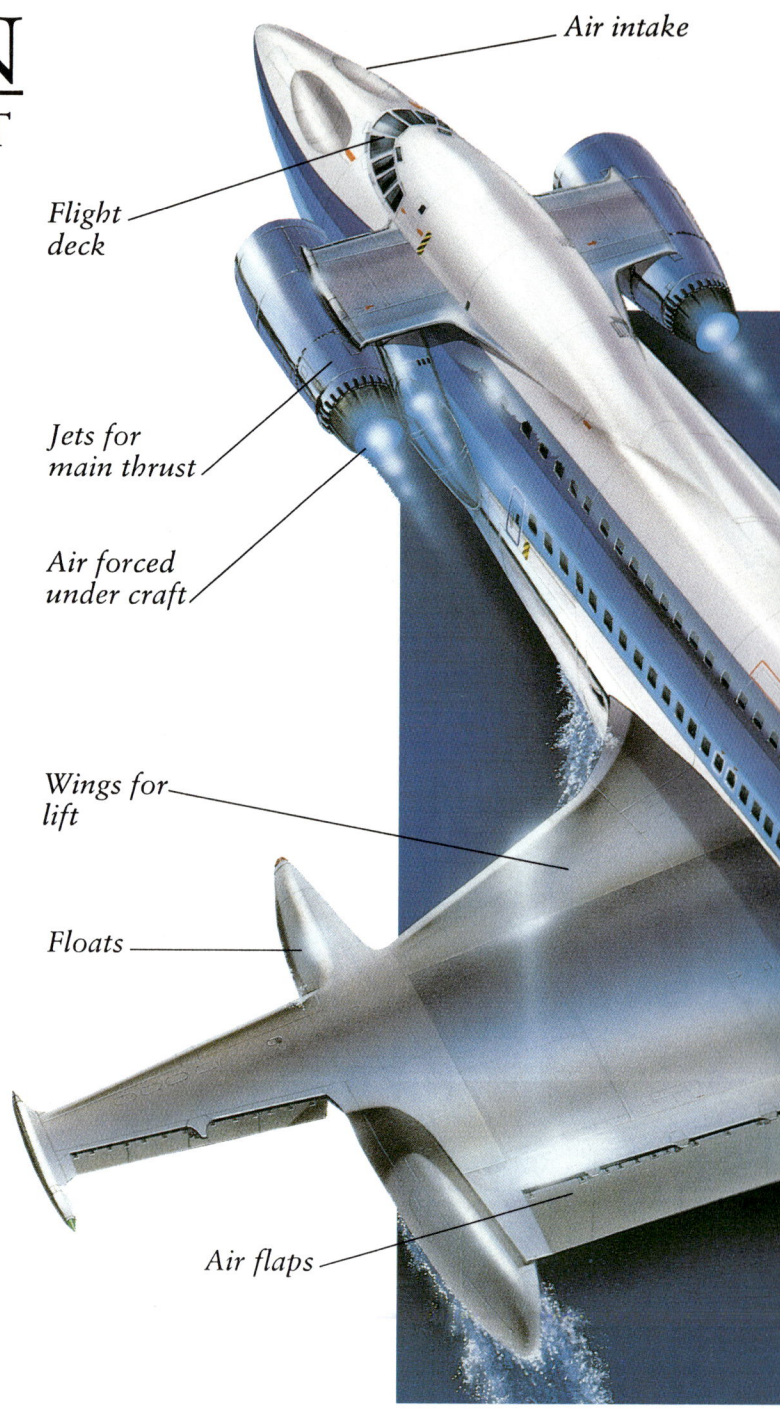

Air intake

Flight deck

Jets for main thrust

Air forced under craft

Wings for lift

Floats

Air flaps

The Airfoil is a new type of boat that is currently being developed in Germany. It uses the same kind of principles as the Aquatain. Short wings on either side of its hull create lift, and help the craft to rise out of the water altogether and fly through the air!

Aquatain would be 73 metres long, and have a wingspan of 180 feet. Carrying 400 passengers, it could be used for short hops like crossing the Channel, or for long-haul flights. One problem is licensing the craft, since nobody has yet decided if it is an aircraft, or a boat. Although there are models and videos, the craft has yet to be seen in the West.

A CUSHION OF AIR
HOW THE AQUATAIN FLIES

Aquatain could fly above water, land or ice. It would use two sets of engines, one to provide forward propulsion and a second set, angled downwards, to direct thrust under the wings. For take-off, a set of deep flaps, called screens, are lowered from the back of the wings, trapping the exhaust gases from the second set of engines and creating a region of compressed air which has the effect of lifting the aircraft away from the water. The forward engines are started, and the craft moves forward, enabling the lift engines to be switched off. The short, broad wings maintain the air cushion on which the craft floats at a height of 14 metres. If necessary, Aquatain can fly much higher, like a conventional aircraft, to avoid storms, but then it is no more economical than any other aircraft. Because few people have ever seen this craft actually fly, some believe that a prototype may have stalled and sank during a trial flight.

The craft was designed by the Russian Hydrofoil Research Centre, and the Soviet Navy has designed several versions. Now the designers want to create a 254-tonne craft able to carry 400 passengers at 482 kph, over distances of up to 17,000 km. This is possible, according to designer Dr Boris Chubikov, because the craft uses only a fifth as much fuel as a conventional aircraft.

When cruising above the sea, propulsion is provided by two front engines.

Take-off is achieved by directing the thrust of the lift engines downwards, using deep flaps or screens at the back of the wings. This creates a cushion of air.

When the craft is aloft, the main engines propel it forward at up to 563 kph, with the wings maintaining the air cushion underneath.

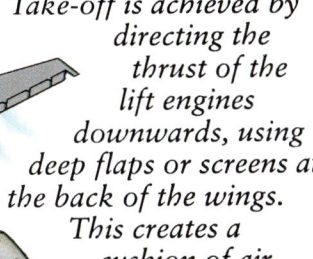

CHRONOLOGY

Ford's Model T

ON THE ROADS

1886 The first cars were developed independently by Gottlieb Daimler and Karl Benz, in Germany. Daimler's Quadricycle had a wooden frame and four wheels, while Benz's Patent Motorwagen was a three-wheeler.

1901 The pattern for the next 40 years was set by the first Mercedes, built by Daimler and Wilhelm Maybach in Germany, and named after the daughter of their sponsor. It had a steel chassis, a four-cylinder engine, and was capable of more than 80 kph.

1908 Popular motoring arrived with Henry Ford's Model T, which used mass production methods to make the car affordable. The Model T appeared in many different shapes over almost 20 years, when 18 million were produced. By 1913, the systems at Ford's Detroit plant enabled a complete Model T to be produced in 93 minutes, and sold for $500.

1911 The Rolls-Royce Silver Ghost set new standards for reliability and comfort. No expense was spared to make it "the best car in the world". To prove how easy it was to drive, one model was driven all the way from London to Edinburgh in top gear.

1924 Ettore Bugatti's Type 35 was a masterpiece of racing-car engineering, beautiful to look at and unbeatable in races. Between 1925 and 1930 the Type 35 carried all before it.

1934 The Citroen 7 was the first car to have front-wheel drive, now almost universal.

1936 The longest-lasting model in the history of motoring is the Volkswagen Beetle, first produced for Adolf Hitler as a car for the people. Its designer was Ferdinand Porsche.

1948 Two famous models made their first appearance: in France the 2CV, and in Britain the Morris Minor. The Morris Minor, designed by Alec Issigonis, though derided by Lord Nuffield as "a poached egg on wheels" contained many innovations.

1959 Issigonis produced the Mini, the car that gave a new word to the language. Its tiny wheels, engine placed

The Mini became a fashionable car in the 1960s

Benz's 3-wheeler from 1888.

sideways, and other innovations alarmed customers, but as soon as the model became a fashionable vehicle its fortune was made.
1981 Daimler-Benz produced the first practical air bag, as a passive safety measure.

BICYCLES
1817 The first attempt at a bicycle was the hobby-horse, invented by Baron Karl Drais von Suaerbronn. The riders could steer, but propelled themselves with their feet on the ground.

1863 Pierre Michaux's Velocipede *had pedals on the front wheels, incorporated a brake, and had a cast-iron frame. Such bikes were then known, as "bone-shakers".*

1870
To go faster, the front wheel needed to become bigger and the result was

the penny-farthing, or the "ordinary" bicycle as it was then called.
1885 The Rover safety bicycle established the shape of the modern bicycle: two wheels of equal size, drive to the rear wheel by chain, a diamond-shaped frame and direct steering by the front wheel.
1889 The Derailleur gear-changing system was invented, and came

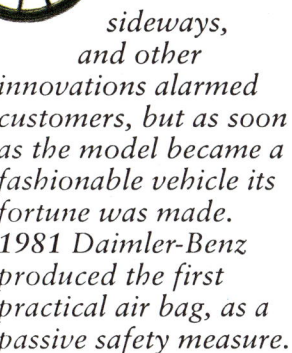

Daimler motorbike

into widespread use after improvements in 1911. It is now the standard gear-change for bikes of all kinds.

MOTORBIKES
1897 The first successful motorbike was produced by Eugene and Michel Werner. It had a motor mounted

in front of the handlebars, driving the front wheel through a leather belt.
1903 The first appearance of the sidecar; though this did not become widely available until 1910.
1988 The first motorbike to boast a reverse gear was the luxurious Honda Goldwing 1500. The reverse was fitted to make manoeuvering the bike easier.

SHIPS AND BOATS
1807 The first successful steamboat was the Clermont, built by the American Robert Fulton in New York. It was 50 metres long, and driven by a steam-powered paddlewheel.

The Mauretania was launched in 1909

Trevithich's Steam Locomotive

1818 The Savannah, *a paddleboat, made the first transatlantic crossing by steam, though for much of the voyage the engines were shut down and the craft propelled by sails.*

1858 Isambard Kingdom Brunel's first great iron ship, the Great Eastern, *used a combination of paddles and screw propulsion, but fuel consumption was so high that the ship proved uneconomic.*

1907 *The first great ocean liners were the* Lusitania, *launched in 1907, and her sister ship the* Mauretania, *launched two years later. Capable of 29.7 knots,* Mauretania *held the Blue Riband for the fastest Atlantic crossing for more than 20 years.*

1936 The Queen Mary *and her sister ship the* Queen Elizabeth *began service just before the Second World War, and soon were converted into troopships. Only the* Queen Mary, *survives, at Long Beach, California.*

1959 *The world's first hovercraft, the SRN-1, was designed and built by British inventor Christopher Cockerell. He decided that the best way to make a boat go faster was to raise it up, supported on a cushion of air.*

RAILWAYS

1804 Richard Trevithick *designed the first steam locomotive to run on rails.*

1829 Stephenson's Rocket, *won a competition on the railway between Liverpool and Manchester. There were six competitors, including one powered by two horses walking on an endless platform like the tracks of a tank, and one man-powered vehicle. Stephenson's* Rocket *covered the 51 kilometres when pulling a train three times its own weight.*

1863 *The Metropolitan Railway, running between Paddington and Farringdon Street, via Euston and King's Cross, became the world's first underground railway.*

Although the locomotives were designed to produce a minimum of smoke, the pollution in the tunnels was dreadful.

1900 *Electrification of the railways began on the Paris-Orleans line. Today all the world's fastest trains use electric propulsion.*

1912 *Sulzer, the Swiss engineering firm, built the first diesel locomotive. The following year, a diesel railcar began operating successfully in Sweden.*

1938 Mallard, *a streamlined Pacific-type locomotive, set the all-time record for steam power, 201 kph.*

1981 *French TGV (Train à grand vitesse) began service between Paris and Lyons. On 26 February the TGV set a record of 423 kph.*

1990 The TGV Atlantique, *an improved version, set a new speed record of 513 km/h on the line near Tours.*

U.S. Naval Hovercraft

GLOSSARY

Articulated
A type of truck made in two parts, a tractor and a trailer unit, connected by a link that can swivel when cornering.

Brake Horsepower (bhp)
The power of a car's engine can be expressed in bhp or kilowatts. 1 bhp is equivalent to 0.746 kilowatts.

Bathyscape
Deep-ocean exploration is made in very strong, often spherical vessels, designed to resist the immense pressures.

Carbon fibre
Thin fibres of carbon which are immenesely strong; usually used as a reinforcement in plastics, to form materials as strong as steel but much lighter.

Downforce
Fast cars can take off, like aircraft, at high speed unless they are designed so that the air flowing over the car forces them downward on to the road.

Drag
The wind-resistance on a moving vehicle is called drag. It increases rapidly as the speed of the vehicle rises.

Emission standards
Limits set on the amount of pollutants, like nitrogen oxides, carbon monoxide and hydrocarbons, that vehicles can emit.

Fairing
Protective bodywork, often of plastic materials which is used on motorbikes to keep rain from the rider's body.

Gas turbine
An engine in which burning fuel drives a turbine: used to power jets, helicopters, and some power stations.

Hybrid cars
Vehicles in which a combination of electrical and conventional motors is used. Hybrid cars could be more economical and cleaner than today's models.

Space frame
Bodywork in which the strength comes from a network of thin tubes welded together to make a rigid frame.

Spoiler
Small wing placed at the back of a car to prevent airflow producing lift, and to create downforce.

Supercharger
Pump for blowing fuel/air mixture into an engine, increasing power. Turbochargers are superchargers that are driven by the flow of exhaust gases.

Superconductivity
The loss of all electrical resistance in a conductor at very low temperatures. Once a current is flowing around a supercondutor it will flow for ever.

Suspension
Arrangement for connecting the wheels of a vehicle to its body, to allow movement as the vehicle crosses rough ground.

INDEX

bicycles
  Behemoth 7
  brakes and gears 6, 29
  carbon-fibre 6, 31
  clipless pedals 6
  designing 6
  frame 6, 7
  handlebars 6
  history 29
  Lotus bike 6, 7
  mountain bikes 7
  optimum airflow 6, 7
  racing bikes 6, 7
  suspension 6, 7
  Zike 6

buses 17

cars
  air bags 11, 29
  batteries 12, 13
  computer-aided design 13
  concept cars 10, 12, 13
  economy cars 12-13
  electric cars 12-13
  engines 12, 15
  hybrid cars 12, 13, 31
  McLaren F1 15
  onboard computers 10, 15
  parking 10
  "platooning" 10
  racing cars 14-15
  "road pricing" systems 11
  route-planners 10
  safety features 10, 11, 14
  seat belts 11
  spoilers 15, 31

catamarans
  speed 20
  stabilisation system 20
  twin hulls 20, 21

coaches 17

computer-aided design
  cars 13
  ships 21

engines
  coaches 17
  diesel 16
  economy cars 12
  racing cars 15
  rotary 9

flying boats 26-7

fuel consumption
  coaches 17
  motorcycles 8

Maglev (magnetically levitated) trains 18-19

motorcycles
  BMW C1 prototype 8
  fuel consumption 8
  history 29
  rotary engine 9
  safety features 8
  steering 8
  suspension 8, 9

ships and boats
  catamarans 20-1
  electromagnetic propulsion 22-3
  flying boats 26-7

  history 29-30
  hovercraft 30
  ocean liners 30
  sail-power 22
  "stealth" ships 20
  steamboats 29-30
  submarines 24-5
  Titanic 24, 25
  Yamato 1 22-3

submarines
  bathyscape 25, 31
  buoyancy 25
  tourist submarines 24, 25
  unmanned submersibles 25

trains
  conventional trains 18
  diesel locomotives 30
  high-speed trains 18-19, 30
  history 30
  magnetically levitated (Maglev) trains 18-19
  SNCF 18
  steam trains 30
  TGV 18, 30
  underground railways 30

trucks
  anti-lock braking systems 16
  "cabover" design 16
  engines 16
  new designs 17
  turning circle 17

wind tunnel tests 6, 7, 15